100 Excuses for Kids

by
Mike Joyer
&
Zach Robert

KNIGHT BOOKS
Hodder and Stoughton

Copyright © 1990 by Beyond Words Publishing, Inc.

First published in Great Britain in 1991 by Knight Books

The rights of Mike Joyer and Zach Robert to be identified as the authors of this work and of Kathleen Jones to be identified as the illustrator of this work, have been asserted by them in accordance with the Copyright, Designs and Patents Act 1988.

Printed and bound in Great Britain for Hodder and Stoughton Children's Books, a division of Hodder and Stoughton Ltd, Mill Road, Dunton Green, Sevenoaks, Kent TN13 2YA. (Editorial Office: 47 Bedford Square, London WC1B 3DP) by Cox & Wyman Ltd, Reading, Berks. Photoset by Rowland Phototypesetting Ltd, Bury St Edmunds, Suffolk.

British Library C.I.P.

Joyer, Mike
  100 excuses for kids.
  I. Title   II. Robert, Zach
827

  ISBN 0-340-54817-7

About the Authors

Co-authors Mike Joyer and Zach Robert are ten and eleven years old, respectively, and have been best friends since they were six.

This is their first book and, for both boys, it is a dream come true.

Mike likes to make people laugh and wants to be a writer and an inventor.

Zach also wants to be a writer, but hopes to be a successful football player first.

Dedication

This book is dedicated to our Mums for encouraging us to finish this book because sometimes we had great excuses not to!

How to Use This Book

If you wish to keep a record of your success with the excuses in this book, fill out the information at the end of the book. Fill in the name of the person you told the excuse to and when. You may also wish to record the results to know whether or not the excuse worked and if you wish to try it again or feel you better not.

Are you ready to have fun with your parents?

This is a book about excuses that you can try on your parents, teachers, and other grown-ups. And we guarantee that you'll have a good laugh.

These are all funny things that we have thought of and we know other kids will enjoy them too.

Grown-ups reading this book may even find something familiar from when they were little and maybe a few excuses they never tried.

So have fun!

Mike & Zach

Table of Contents

Excuses

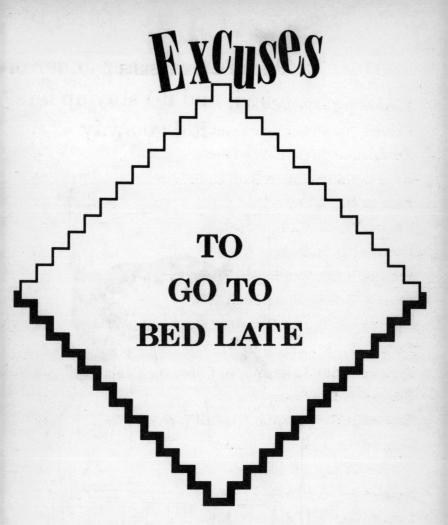

TO
GO TO
BED LATE

Mike: Zach and I are night owls. We'd both go to bed around 11:30 or 12 if we had our choice. I'd spend the extra time watching TV or reading a book, and Zach would read or draw. These excuses work best if you just use them once in a while. Otherwise, you get too tired and can't keep your excuses straight.

There's a monster under my
bed, and if I stay up late
it'll go away.

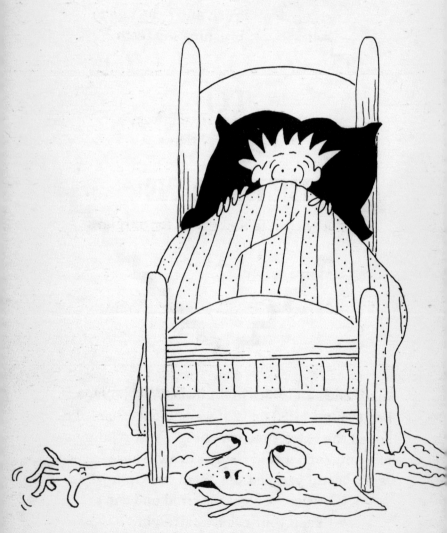

I lost my toothbrush and I can't go to
bed without brushing my teeth.

◆

If I go to bed early, I'll forget
everything I know.

◆

I'll stay up late and watch for burglars.

◆

If I stay up late, I can tuck you in.

◆

I'm doing research on late night television.

If I stay up late, I can tell you a good night story.

◆

If I stay up late, I'll make you a midnight snack.

◆

I don't need my beauty sleep, I'm
already too beautiful.

◆

If I stay up late, I might see a shooting star!

What's your **E**x**C**u**s**e**?**

I'll stay off school
if you don't let me stay
up late at night

Excuses

NOT TO
EAT YOUR
VEGETABLES

Zach: My least favourite foods are lima beans,
mushrooms, tomatoes and onions. My mum
makes me eat them unless I can come up
with a nifty excuse.

I'm allergic to vegetables.

My vegies lost all their nutrition.

◆

I'm going to donate my vegies to the poor.

◆

Vegetables are for vegetarians.

◆

I only eat cherry-flavoured vegies.

◆

I don't need them — I ate some last month.

I just saw a worm crawl out of my vegies!

♦

You put too much pepper in my vegetables.

♦

The tin that the vegies came in was dented!

♦

Once there was a man that ate too
many vegetables and lost all his hair!

What's your **Excuse?**

I don't eat vegies I am
a meatatarian

ExCuses

NOT TO GO TO THE DENTIST

Mike: Kids really do have to go to the dentist regularly. We know that. You can have some fun with these excuses — just don't expect them all to work!

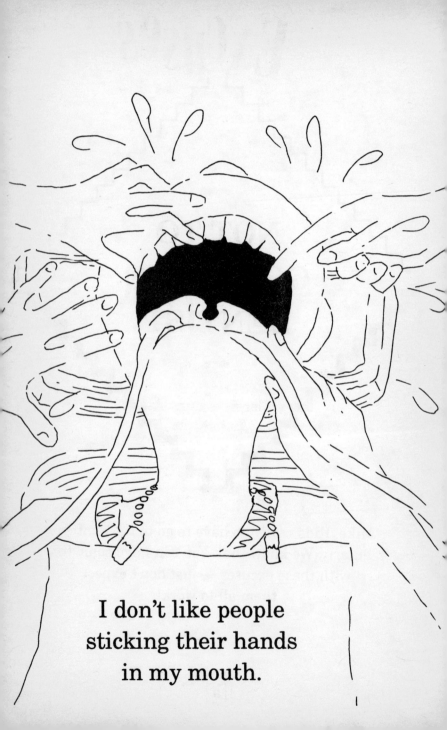

I don't like people
sticking their hands
in my mouth.

My friend went to the dentist and
his teeth fell out!

◆

He always misses my teeth and
works on my nose!

◆

I'm allergic to dentists.

◆

I'd rather work on my own teeth.

But Christopher Columbus never
went to the dentist.

◆

I don't need all those teeth anyway!

◆

My toothpaste cleans my teeth for me.

What's your Excuse?

the dentist's moustash
always tickels my nose

Excuses

NOT TO
TAKE A BATH
OR SHOWER

Zach: I think kids should only have to take a bath
every other day, or every three days. Mike
thinks he should only have to take one
when he wants to get warm. Try these excuses
and see if you can take fewer baths.

Our
hot
water
doesn't
work!

When I'm about to take a shower, spiders come out of the plug hole.

◆

But when I take a bath (or shower), the water rates go up.

◆

Every time I take a shower the bathroom gets flooded.

◆

The water comes down so hard it makes dents in my head!

◆

But if I take a bath the steam will make the paint peel.

Too much water will rust the pipes.

◆

But I might shrink!

◆

I look good in dirt.

◆

But I'm so dirty the dirt will clog the drain.

What's your Excuse?

I had a bath (or shower) when
I came in from school

EXCUSES

NOT TO DRESS SMARTLY

My favourite excuse is that my clothes are dirty.
Once I made my excuse come to life: I took my clean
clothes and I put them in the wash, and said they
were dirty. I wouldn't recommend doing this.

My clothes are
    too big
    for me!

Someone cut my clothes up!

◆

Someone forgot to wash my clothes.

◆

I'm too fat and my clothes won't fit.

◆

My clothes are stuck under my bed.

◆

There's a hole in my shirt.

What's your **Excuse?**

_____

I can't find my clothes

_____

_____

_____

Excuses

NOT TO CLEAN YOUR ROOM

Zach: Sometimes you might have to do another kind of job to get out of this one, but if your room is anything like mine, it could be worth it.

I planned on cleaning my room tomorrow.

◆

I need to finish my homework.

◆

If I clean my room I won't know where anything is!

◆

I cleaned my room a year ago.

What's your ExCuse?

_____

I might trip over
something while im
tidying up and break my
leg.

EXCUSES

NOT TO DO YOUR HOMEWORK

Mike: Some of these excuses can be used with teachers as well as parents. Just remember not to use the same one too many times. I mean, how often can the dog eat your homework?

The dog ate my homework!

Homework strains my eyes.

◆

I lost my homework on the way home from school.

◆

I forgot what my homework was.

◆

A bully took my books.

It was cold outside, and I built a fire
out of my homework.

◆

I shredded up my books and recycled
them for paper.

◆

But everytime I try to write,
the lead keeps coming out of my pencil.

◆

It was so windy outside that my books
flew into a passing car!

What's your **Excuse?**

I feel to ill to do
my homework.

Excuses

TO GET YOUR POCKET-MONEY INCREASED

Zach: Well, these are good for a laugh, anyway!

If I get more money,
I can buy you
something
special.

I'll save my pocket-money for college.

◆

With the pocket-money I get now,
I can't even buy a stick of chewing-gum!

◆

I'll work twice as hard for more money.

◆

I'll treat everyone to a pizza!

What's your **Excuse?**

_the other kids at school
get much more money
than I do_

29

Excuses

TO STAY HOME FROM SCHOOL

Mike: Use these with caution. Remember,
sometimes staying home can turn out to be boring.

My socks don't match!

I lost all my pencils and I have to stay at home
and look for them.

◆

If I go to school, I'll forget
everything I know from home.

◆

The teachers are on strike.

◆

School gives me learning cramps.

What's your EXCUSE?

Our techer gives us to
much work, and if I work too
hard I might faint

Excuses

NOT TO PLAY WITH YOUR BROTHER OR SISTER

Zach: Mike has a sister and I have a brother, so we're experts on this subject. These excuses can be used for either brothers or sisters.

He
screams
and
yells
at
me.

She always ruins the game.

◆

He slobbers on me.

◆

She runs around and trips over things,
and I don't want her to get hurt.

◆

I'm already booked to
play with somebody else's brother/sister.

It'll be good for her to learn to play by herself.

◆

He will colour all over the wall.

◆

I played with her last week.

What's your Excuse?

She/he is at a friends
house so I can't play
with him/her

EXCUSES

TO GO
FISHING

Mike: These excuses work really well. The only problem is, once you go fishing and catch some fish, you have to think of an excuse not to clean them.

They've
got
the
biggest
fish
in the
world
in
this
pond!

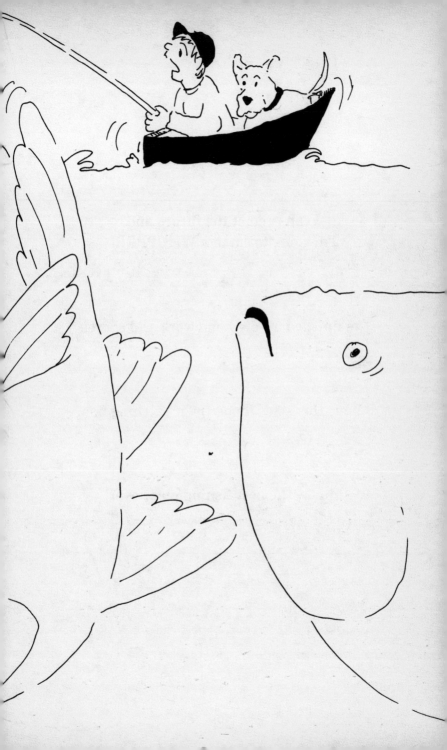

I can predict the future and
I'm going to catch a WHOPPER!

◆

I've finished all my homework and chores.

◆

I have this special power for catching fish.

◆

I know the best fishing place ever!

My bait is going to rot if I don't use it quickly.

◆

I have to do a report on fish so I have to catch one to study.

◆

You look hungry, so I'll catch some fish.

◆

I think Salmon is a pretty colour so I want to hang one on my wall.

What's your Excuse?

I will catch a big fish for your tea if you let me go fishing

Excuses

TO BUY SWEETS AT THE CHECK-OUT COUNTER

Zach: There are a lot of different ways for using these excuses. I recommend starting them early in the shopping trip, when you have more time to work on your mums or dads — and they have more money.

This is the last time
I'll ever ask you!

Sweets will give me energy to help carry the shopping!

◆

I feel weak with hunger!

◆

I won't ask for anything for the rest of the year!

◆

I need the wrappers to win the £1000 competition!

What's your **Excuse?**

I'll buy you some
as well.

Excuses

**TO BUY
SUGAR-COATED
CEREAL**

Mike: If all else fails, you could offer to
use sugar-coated cereal as a dessert.

But there's a great toy inside!

This cereal has vitamins in it!

◆

<u>Graeme</u> eats it every day, and
he's/she's the strongest person in the class!

◆

We have a coupon for it!

◆

I won't have dessert for a month!

What's your Excuse?

theres a great prize
inside for mums and
dads

Excuses

TO GET YOUR MUM OR DAD TO ORDER PIZZAS!

Zach: It's usually not too hard to talk your parents into ordering pizzas. In fact, sometimes all they need is a good excuse.

A giant came bursting in here and ate all the food!

◆

Pizza is good for you. It has the four food groups,
if we get pineapple, too!

◆

But the pizza place delivers it to us!

◆

Think of all those poor
delivery people that need a job!

What's your Excuse?

it will make me
big and strong so that
I can help you with the
house work

ExCuses

NOT TO DO
YOUR CHORES

Mike: These excuses help put off your chores.
We couldn't think of too many good ones
for getting out of doing them.

I can't do my chores
right now. I'm waiting
for my hair to grow!

I can't do them right now. I have to finish my homework!

◆

I can't do them right now because I have to go out and get some exercise!

◆

I'll do them tomorrow. I'm too busy today!

I'm so tired out from yesterday's chores,
I can't do them today!

I played hard all day. I'll have
more energy tomorrow.

What's your Excuse?

if you let me have
time to not do my
chores. for the rest of
the week. I will do
my sisters chores
next week

ExCuSeS

TO OPEN
YOUR PRESENTS
EARLY

Zach: Sometimes it helps to pretend you
have a good motive, like saying you want to start
your thank-you letters early.

I just saw something move in that present, and I have to open it!

If you don't want me to open it, I'll go into the other room where you can't see me!

◆

It's already _____ on the other side of the world!

◆

Just this once, can I open presents before cake and ice cream?

◆

I can get started on my thank-you letters early!

What's your **Excuse?**

_____

I will give you an

extra prensent on your

birthday

Excuses

TO GET YOUR POCKET-MONEY EARLY

Mike: Zach's brother gets his pocket-money early by sneaking a toy he wants into the shopping trolley when his mum isn't looking. By the time she notices, it's too late and she's already bought it. So then she makes him pay for it out of his pocket-money and he has to get it early to pay her.

Zach and I think this may be going too far.

I'll do extra chores if you give it to me now!

◆

I'll empty the rubbish bins two extra times!

◆

Will you give me my pocket-money
early because you love me?

◆

If I don't get my pocket-money now,
this toy will sell out.

What's your Excuse?

all the other kids
at school get their
pocket money early

ExCuses

TO PLAY
VIDEO GAMES

Zach: I think kids should do whatever they
have to do first before asking to play video games,
because, otherwise, you get hooked on it and
it's hard to stop and do something else.

My hands are stuck
to the control.
I CAN'T MOVE!

I've gone blind! I can't see anything but ZELDA!

◆

This is my most interesting game.
I can't put it down!

◆

An avalanche blocked the way out of my room!

◆

But I thought you told me to go and "play"!

What's your **Excuse?**

My friend wanted to see
another video game so I have
to finish this video game
first.

Excuses

TO KEEP VISITORS OUT OF YOUR ROOM

Mike: These are excuses to keep people like relatives from sleeping in your room when they come to stay with you. Sometimes I don't mind letting visitors use my bedroom, if I can sleep in the front room and make houses and fortresses out of the blankets and the furniture.

IT'S
HAUNTED!

My room's too small!

◆

My room will soon be condemned. I'm very sorry!

◆

Blow me bagpipes! My room just CAVED IN!

◆

The salad I had last week is all over the floor!

◆

There's glue on the floor!

My friend's too ugly to be seen and he's in there.

◆

My room . . . . . IT VANISHED!

◆

There is no vacancy at this time!

What's your **Excuse?**

My room has something
secret in it and nobody
can see what it is sorry

EXCUSES

TO BUY SWEETS

Zach: If you use these excuses too often, you'll have to polish up your excuses for not going to the dentist.

It was made in the UK!

◆

It's in my favourite shapes!

◆

It comes with free balloons!

◆

The more sugar I eat, the sweeter I get!

◆

I'll buy you some!

What's your **Excuse?**

The prime minister said
anybody who doesn't
eat sweets today will be
put in jail

EXCUSES

**NOT TO
GET YOUR
HAIR CUT**

Mike: If these don't work, you can always say long
hair is coming back in style.

When my hair is longer,
I can see better!

My friends will laugh at me if they see my hair, so I have to get it cut when summer comes!

♦

My friends and I are having a contest to see who can grow the longest hair!

♦

I like my hair how it is!

♦

All the barbers in the nation cut it TOO short!

♦

My hair is too thin. It can't be cut!

What's your **Excuse?**

I won't look nice
with short hair.

Excuses

TO WATCH
MORE TV

Zach: Your parents may remember using some of
these excuses themselves. Butter them up by using
the last excuse — the one about wanting to watch
the shows that were on when they were children.

My chores and homework are finished!

◆

A special programme is coming on and
I have to watch it for school!

◆

I can do my homework
better when the TV is on!

◆

I have to do a report on commercials, so
I have to watch TV!

◆

My brain has a mental block and TV helps me to
get rid of that!

◆

TV shows me how to play sports better!

All my favourite stars are in this show,
so I have to watch it!

◆

I haven't watched TV for at least 10 hours,
so I NEED to watch it now!

◆

There's a classic on that you used to watch
and I want to see what you saw when you were
young!

What's your **Excuse?**

I am doing a project on
t.v. so I have to watch
t.v.

ExCuses

TO GO
SKIING

Mike: It helps if your parents like to ski.

I want to try out for the Olympic Ski Team.

It builds strong leg muscles and I need stronger muscles to run faster!

◆

I need fresh air and skiing gives me fresh air!

◆

It's supposed to be a nice day tomorrow and we don't want to waste a nice day!

◆

We have a lot of spare money and we can go to ___Olympia___ (name a ski resort)!

What's your EXCUSE?

its the winter holidays and there is nothing else to do.

ExCuses

TO GO TO
A FUN FAIR

This is really tough, because most parents hate
fun fairs. You really have to tell them how going
to one will make you braver and richer.

I'm feeling lucky on the slot machines.

Dodgems will help me learn to drive!

◆

The big wheel and switchback will make me brave.

◆

It's FUN!

◆

They have the best hot dogs there!

What's your Excuse?

_____

everyone else is going

_____

_____

MY BEST EXCUSES:

Excuse   **Who/When**

_____

_____

_____

_____

_____

_____

_____

_____

_____

_____

_____

_____

_____

_____

_____

_____

Worked	Didn't Work	Try Again	DON'T

A complete list of the FAMOUS FIVE ADVENTURES
by Enid Blyton

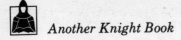 *Another Knight Book*

Rolf Harris

YOUR CARTOON TIME

Did you know that you can draw?

Rolf Harris shows you how – clearly and simply – in
Your Cartoon Time.
Starting with stick figures, he explains how to develop
these step-by-step into your own stylish characters,
and there are ideas too for how you can use your
drawings – as birthday cards, home movies and so on.

Drawing is fun!

All you need is a pencil, paper and Rolf Harris's book
– *Your Cartoon Time*.

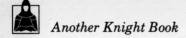 *Another Knight Book*

Allan Rune Pettersson

FRANKENSTEIN'S AUNT

"Next stop Frankenstein!" Aunt Frankenstein has
arrived determined to restore her nephew's devastated
castle to order and clear the family's blackened name!
An hilariously spooky sequel to the famous
Frankenstein story.

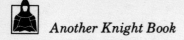
Another Knight Book

Jeremy Tapscott

THE INTER GALACTIC JOKE BOOK

Are you spaced out or simply astronuts? Yes? Then put on your Apollo-neck jumper and launch yourself up to planet humour with *The Inter Galactic Joke Book*.

To boldly joke, where no man has joked before! Every space joke under the sun, and a whole lot from even further on. Every one guaranteed to put you into orbit. You'll be glad you bought this joke book. In fact, you'll be over the moon.

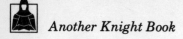

Another Knight Book

Gyles Brandreth

MY RECORD BOOK

The pogo bouncing, baked bean picking,
wellie-wanging, jolly jelly record book!

How many pairs of socks can *you* put on, one on top of
another? Can *you* eat an entire tin of baked beans in
19 minutes using only a cocktail stick? And what
exactly *are* the credentials for being a record-breaker?

YOU'D BETTER GET A COPY AT RECORD SPEED
AND FIND OUT!